Scholastic BookFiles

A READING GUIDE TO

Holes

by Louis Sachar

Monique Vescia

Library of Congress Cataloging-in-Publication Data
Vescia, Monique.
Scholastic BookFiles: A Reading Guide to Holes
by Louis Sachar/by Monique Vescia.
p. cm.
Summary: Discusses the writing, characters, plot, and themes of this 1999 Newbery Award–winning book. Includes discussion questions and activities. Includes bibliographical references (p.).
1. Sachar, Louis, 1954– . Holes—Juvenile literature.
2. Homeless persons in literature—Juvenile literature.
3. Friendship in literature—Juvenile literature.
4. Boys in literature—Juvenile literature.   [1. Sachar, Louis, 1954– . Holes.   2. American literature—History and criticism.]
I. Title: A Reading Guide to Holes by Louis Sachar.   II. Title.
PS3569.A226 H6538 2003
813′.54—dc21   2002191229

0-439-46336-X

10 9 8 7 6 5   03 04 05 06 07

Composition by Brad Walrod/High Text Graphics, Inc.
Cover and interior design by Red Herring Design

Printed in the U.S.A.   23
First printing, July 2003

Contents

About Louis Sachar

"I want kids to think that reading can be just as much fun and more so than TV or video games or whatever else they do."

—Louis Sachar

Holes tells the story of how a single event—a pair of sneakers falling out of the sky—changes the course of a person's life. Author Louis Sachar knows a thing or two about that: In college he signed up for a job as a teacher's aide at an elementary school because he thought it sounded easy. As it turned out, the time Sachar spent working with the kids at Hillside Elementary School in California inspired him to try writing children's books. Now he's an award-winning author!

Louis Sachar (pronounced *Sacker*) was born in East Meadow, New York, on March 20, 1954. Sachar's mother stayed at home to care for Louis and his older brother, Andy. Their father commuted to New York City to work on the seventy-eighth floor of the Empire State Building. Sachar's father sold Italian shoes, which may help explain the strange significance of footwear in the plot of *Holes*.

As a kid, Sachar remembers trying to fit in. He played in the Little League, ran track when he was in middle school, and was a good student. He liked reading books, especially those by E. B. White, who wrote *Charlotte's Web* and *Stuart Little.* Sachar also recalls having to stay clear of the woods across the street from his house where the older, tougher kids liked to play. When he was nine, his family moved west, to a town called Tustin in southern California.

"Writing was always my first love," Sachar insists, but he worked at a variety of other jobs before becoming an author. He even had a short but surprisingly successful career as a Fuller Brush Man, selling scrub brushes and other household items door-to-door.

Sachar went to college at the University of California at Berkeley, where he majored in economics. He graduated in 1976. After college, Sachar worked in a sweater warehouse in Norwalk, Connecticut, and wrote at night. He continued writing even after he enrolled in school to become a lawyer. In fact, it was during his first week in law school that Sachar got the news that his first book, *Sideways Stories from Wayside School* (1978), had been accepted for publication. After graduating from law school, Sachar worked part-time as a lawyer for eight years while he continued writing children's books. He finally quit practicing law in 1989 to become a full-time writer.

To date, Sachar has published twenty-one books for children. He clearly has a gift for creating memorable characters that readers want to hear more about. Sachar's first book, *Sideways Stories from Wayside School*, evolved into a series of zany tales about a school accidentally built sideways, that is, thirty stories tall with one class on each floor. Sachar has also written a series of books featuring a character named Marvin Redpost, a boy who believes he is actually a prince who was kidnapped at birth. *Holes*, a more complex and ambitious book than Sachar's earlier works, was published in 1998.

Sachar's editor Frances Foster has compared his success to that of Roald Dahl, the author of *Charlie and the Chocolate Factory* and *James and the Giant Peach*. "Louis was discovered by the children who loved his books, like the Wayside stories. There are books which adults discover and push onto kids—this was completely the other way around." It's easy to see why the absurd humor of a book like *Sideways Stories from Wayside School* would appeal to young readers: In one chapter, a smelly new student turns out to be a dead rat dressed in layers of overcoats!

Sachar's books have won many awards. *Holes* earned a dozen honors and became the first book ever to win both the Newbery Medal and the National Book Award for Young People's Literature in the same year. The Newbery, the most prestigious prize in American literature for children, is awarded annually by the children's librarians of the American Library Association. Another great honor, the National Book Award, is presented to one book each year selected by the National Book Foundation as an outstanding contribution to children's literature. Sachar receives a lot of fan letters from readers who have enjoyed his books, and he visits schools and bookstores all over the country where he reads and talks about his work.

Sachar currently lives in Austin, Texas. He met his wife, Carla, while visiting an elementary school where she worked as a counselor. Their daughter, Sherre, was born in 1987. Sachar enjoys playing chess, tennis, and tournament bridge. He also likes to ski and play guitar. He has two dogs named Tippy and Lucky. They are the only company allowed in his office while he is writing.

"It took me a year and a half to write
<u>Holes</u>, and nobody knew anything about
it, not even my wife or my daughter."

—Louis Sachar

If Louis Sachar had never moved to Texas—if he had stayed on the East Coast where he was born or in California where he went to school—there's a good chance *Holes* might never have been written. In his acceptance speech for the *Boston Globe–Horn Book* Award, one of the many prizes he has won for the book, Sachar told the audience, "*Holes* was inspired by my dislike of the hot Texas summer." Luckily, Sachar was in the right place at the right time to dream up this award-winning tale. In contrast, the unlikely hero of the darkly humorous story seems to always be in the wrong place at the wrong time. Then again, if Stanley hadn't walked under that freeway overpass at just the right moment . . . well, who knows what might have happened to him? "When the shoes first fell from the sky, [Stanley] remembered thinking that destiny had struck him."

Sachar spent eighteen months writing *Holes*, which, coincidentally, is the length of Stanley's sentence at Camp Green Lake. Sometimes the work of bringing this wonderful story to light seemed like hard labor to its creator: "As I was writing the novel, I identified with my main character, Stanley Yelnats, who had to dig a hole each day, five feet deep and five feet wide, under the blazing Texas sun. Most days I, too, felt like I was struggling for no apparent reason." As is his practice, Sachar kept all of the details about the book to himself until he finished it. "By not permitting myself to talk about *Holes*, I was forced to write it. The story was growing inside me for a year and a half, and I had no other way to let it out."

Every writer has his or her influences, and two books in particular provided inspiration for this one: Kurt Vonnegut's *Hocus Pocus* and William Goldman's *The Princess Bride*. As Sachar told the *Austin Chronicle*, "I like the way the opening chapters [of *Hocus Pocus*] were sort of short and jumpy, and how they led into the story. . . . And *The Princess Bride* had these colorful characters and this bizarre setting, and that's sort of like *Holes*."

Holes was first published in 1998, when Sachar's daughter, Sherre, was in fourth grade. She told her father she thought the Warden, the mysterious red-haired woman in charge of Camp Green Lake, was scary. Sachar was surprised when other readers agreed. He'd imagined the Warden, with her venomous fingernails, as a cartoonish and exaggerated villain, like the characters in comic books. Sachar says he based the figure of the Warden on a woman he knows. "But she's not nasty like the Warden, not at all. She's very nice." All the other characters and events in *Holes* come from Sachar's imagination, including the yellow-spotted lizards that play such an important role in the story.

During his career as an author, Sachar has invented many memorable characters, which have reappeared in later books in the Wayside School and Marvin Redpost series. The plot structure of *Holes* makes the possibility of a sequel unlikely, however. The lifting of the Yelnats family curse and the closure of Camp Green Lake suggest we will not be hearing any more about Stanley Yelnats. As the narrator of *Holes* says at the novel's conclusion, "You will have to fill in the holes yourself."

◆ *In* Holes, *the character of X-Ray says that every kid in the world wants to dig a big hole. Was this true of you? Did you ever do it?*

No, but the idea of it sounded like fun.

About being a writer

◆ *What experience—or maybe it was a person or a teacher—first encouraged you to imagine yourself as a writer?*

I think it was in high school that I [learned to like] to write. Probably because my brother did. I don't think any teacher in particular directed me that way. If I was influenced by anyone, I guess it was by J. D. Salinger and Kurt Vonnegut, the authors I was reading at that time.

◆ *Were little stories and stuff like that the first things you remember enjoying writing?*

Yeah, I took a creative writing class when I was a senior in high school.

Do you think that was worthwhile? There's always that question of whether you can teach writing.

Oh, I think it was very worthwhile, not so much because of anything the teacher taught us but because we had to write a story every week or every two weeks and because every time you write you learn from your writing.

How do you prepare to write a book? Do you keep notes or a journal, or do any particular kind of research?

No. I sit at my desk and think, Oh, what am I going to do? [Sachar laughs.] It's a real slow process, and I might go week after week and not be able to come up with anything that interests me enough to sit down and write about. So . . . there are a lot of days where I feel like I just can't think of anything. And at some point I get an idea and I start to explore it and write a little bit about it and it grows, and new ideas spring from that, and that's how the story gets started.

Many of your books have evolved into sequels. What are some of the pleasures of writing about the same characters in many different situations, and what are some of the difficulties of that?

To me the most fun part of writing is creating the new characters. Sequels are less enjoyable to write, but in a lot of ways they're easier because you already know the characters.

◆ Are you encouraged, in part, to write sequels by the response of your readers who want to hear more about those characters?

That was definitely the case with [the] Wayside School [series]. *Marvin Redpost* was always written with the idea that there would be several of them. And then one of my very early books was *Someday, Angeline,* and with that one I really liked all the characters a lot but when I looked back on it years later I didn't really think the story was all that engaging. And so I thought I would try to give those characters another chance. So . . . the same characters are in the book *Dogs Don't Tell Jokes.*

◆ What's the nicest compliment you've ever received as a writer? Besides, of course, winning the Newbery and all those other awards!

Well, I hear all the time from kids or from parents who tell me their kids never liked to read and then all of a sudden they read one of my books and they can't stop. I've heard that a lot and that always feels really good.

◆ Do you read reviews of your work?

I read them. I mean, I'm always curious what people think and also what reviewers think because other people are going to read that. Reviews don't necessarily influence anything I write. But often I've been very impressed by the reviewer because, especially if it's a good review, it can also analyze what I did and I would think, Yeah, that's right, that *is* what I did! I don't analyze what I do when I write. I always did poorly in English classes because I could always sort of internalize a book but I could never say what it was that really moved me about the book. It's the same way with my own writing.

Did winning the Newbery and other awards for Holes *make it difficult to write the next book? Was the next one* Marvin Redpost for Class President*?*

It was, but that was written before all the success of *Holes*. It took a year and a half after I wrote *Holes* before it was published, and during that time I was working on [the] Marvin Redpost [series]. Of course, those were much simpler books. They weren't trying to be as big and as grand as *Holes*.

So you do see Holes *as an ambitious book? Did you feel that way when you were launching yourself into it?*

Yes. I mean, all the other books I'd written had been about kids in school with a familiar background. But this was completely different; the story was all this past history and wide-open adventure. It was a lot different from anything else I'd written. And when I finished writing it and people would ask me, "Is this going to make it hard to write your next book?" I always felt that no, it added to my confidence. But it's been awhile, and I still haven't written that next book! [Sachar laughs.] So I think I do feel the pressure to try to equal *Holes,* to come up with something again that will be big and grand. . . . You know, *Holes* is read by both adults and children, so . . . I feel like, well, do I want to write for children next or do I want to write for adults?

♦ *I imagine Texas probably wants to claim you, but do you see yourself as a part of any regional literary community?*

No. I don't feel like a part of any literary community. I don't meet with other writers. It's just me alone in my room, and then going and speaking at different places around the country.

♦ *Do you enjoy the solitary nature of being a writer? Or is that one of the things that's hard about it?*

Both. I mean, I generally enjoy it and I think I'd have a hard time not having that, but at the same time it does make it difficult to always have to be self-motivated. But for the last year or two I've been working on the movie of *Holes*, and that's meant cooperating with many other people.

Making *Holes* into a movie

♦ *What were some of the challenges of adapting* Holes *for a screenplay?*

The hardest part for me was just being able to see it as a movie . . . to get the rhythm of the movie in your mind instead of the rhythm of the book. And a lot of people, when I mention that [*Holes* was made into] a movie, say to me, "Oh, that's perfect! You know, I visualize it so well when I'm reading the book." But it's different, because a lot of that visualizing they're doing is in their mind. I might have just given a few little clues—saying it's hot, he's thirsty—and then they draw from that this whole picture.

But for the screenplay you have to describe every picture, and you have to do it in a very succinct [brief] way. It's not left to the imagination. You have to tell the director and the actors and the camera what they're looking at, what they're actually seeing. So that was more difficult.

About *Holes*

▶ *At what point in writing* Holes *did you decide that your protagonist would have a palindrome for a name?*

When I first came up with the name, it was just something to put down on paper. I didn't feel like thinking of his name, so I just wrote *Stanley* and then wrote it backwards. I always figured I would change it. [But] at some point into the story... I thought that I wasn't going to change it. I liked the fact that it gave a kind of quirky humor to the beginning of the book. So that even though you knew Stanley was sent to this awful place for a crime he didn't commit, you know right away that it's not going to be just this grim story. And then the other reason I kept the name is because it was an easy way of telling the reader that he had the same name as his father and his grandfather and his great-grandfather, without making it stand out, without [making the reader think], Well, why are you telling me this? Because it's important at the end, you know, that his great-grandfather was also named Stanley. If you just said, Oh, by the way, he has the same name as his great-grandfather, well, who cares? But if you make kind of a joke out of it—that all these people are named because of this palindrome—then you don't realize you're being told this vital piece of information.

*I'm curious about your use of the second-person pronoun in the book (for example, "You are now entering Camp Green Lake....").
Did you decide to write directly to the reader from the beginning, or did that develop as you were writing?*

That emerged as I was working on it. Especially the stuff where I'd say, "'You make the decision: Whom did God punish?'" I kind of surprised myself that I was taking this tone . . . [and using] things like "God's thumb" and "You make the decision"—I mean, it's sort of this very high-handed tone of the writer. And I surprised myself that I took on that tone.

There are a lot of passages in Holes *that are very sad to read. I'm thinking about when Zero is talking about his childhood. Were those parts difficult to write?*

I don't remember. It's all difficult. . . . Whenever I write I try to keep it interesting and entertaining. I don't like reading things that are overly sentimental, so I would never want to write something like that.

You obviously have a knack for creating characters that your readers want to hear more about, and many of your other books are part of a series. Are you planning a sequel to Holes?

[No, but] I've toyed with the idea of writing a story about Armpit or X-Ray.

Finally, I just have to ask this: Do you suffer from foot odor?

No.

Chapter Charter:
Questions to Guide Your Reading

The following questions will help you think about the important parts of each chapter.

Chapter 1

- What do you learn in this chapter about the setting of the story? Based on its name, what would you imagine a place called Camp Green Lake to be like? What is it really like?

Chapter 2

- Do you think it's true that digging holes can turn a bad person into a good one? What are some other unpleasant things you've heard about that are supposed to "build character"?

Chapter 3

- Stanley's father, an inventor, says, "I learn from failure." What do you think this means? Have you ever learned from failure?

Chapter 4

- What kind of tattoo does Mr. Sir have? What does this tell you about him?

Chapter 5

- Why do the boys call Mr. Pendanski "Mom"? Does this nickname suit him?

Chapter 6
- Why don't the boys believe Stanley when he tells them he stole the sneakers?

Chapter 7
- What does Stanley learn from digging his first hole? Why do you think he feels proud when his hole is finished?

Chapter 8
- Do you believe in curses? Why or why not?

Chapter 9
- How do you feel about the nickname X-Ray gives Stanley? Do you have a nickname? If so, how did you get it?

Chapter 10
- Why do the boys always line up for water in the same order? What's the significance to this order?

Chapter 11
- What does X-Ray ask Stanley to do? Why does Stanley agree to this? What would you have done?

Chapter 12
- Mr. Pendanski tells Stanley: "You messed up your life, and it's up to you to fix it." Do you agree with this?

Chapter 13
- What does Stanley gain when he agrees to help X-Ray? What does he lose?

Chapter 14

- Were you surprised to discover that the Warden is a woman? What else do you find out about the Warden in this chapter?

Chapter 15

- Do you think Zigzag and the other campers are correct in believing that the Warden is always watching them, or are they just being paranoid?

Chapter 16

- Can you think of some reasons why Zero might not be familiar with any nursery rhymes or the show *Sesame Street*?

Chapter 17

- What does Stanley find out about Zigzag in this chapter?

Chapter 18

- Why do you think Stanley continues lying to his mom and dad in his letters?

Chapter 19

- Why does Stanley tell Mr. Sir that he stole the sunflower seeds? What would you have done?

Chapter 20

- The Warden does not raise her voice, and she usually speaks in seemingly polite phrases. What makes her so menacing?

Chapter 21

- Why do you think Zero finishes Stanley's hole for him?

Chapter 22

- Does Stanley seem like a good teacher? Have you ever tutored anyone? What did you learn from the experience?

Chapter 23

- Does the portrait the author paints of Green Lake seem realistic? Can you point to any details that strike you as too good to be true?

Chapter 24

- How does Mr. Sir get back at Stanley? Do you think it is Stanley's fault that Mr. Sir got scratched?

Chapter 25

- Does it seem like Sam is a respected member of the Green Lake community? Why or why not?

Chapter 26

- Based on the facts the author gives you, can you answer the question, "Whom did God punish?"

Chapter 27

- Why don't the other boys approve of Stanley and Zero's arrangement? Do you think it is fair to both boys?

Chapter 28

- Who else has turquoise-studded boots like Kate Barlow's?

Chapter 29

- What do you think is the significance of Stanley's vision of the giant thumb?

Chapter 30

- Why doesn't Stanley fight back when Zigzag taunts him? What would you do in his position?

Chapter 31

- Why doesn't Stanley go after Zero?

Chapter 32

- Thinking about Zero, "what worried [Stanley] the most . . . was the fear that it *wasn't* too late." What does this mean?

Chapter 33

- Does Stanley approach his predicament intelligently? Is his logic sound? What would you do in the same situation?

Chapter 34

- When Stanley sees Big Thumb, "[H]e kept walking toward it, although he didn't know why." Why do *you* think Stanley keeps going?

Chapter 35

- How would you describe Stanley and Zero's relationship at this point in the story?

Chapter 36

- What does Stanley learn about himself as they climb the mountain? What does he learn about Zero?

Chapter 37

- Why do you think Stanley suddenly calls Zero Hector?

Chapter 38

- "[Stanley] thought only about each step, and not the impossible task that lay before him." Have you ever attempted anything that seemed impossible? How did you approach it? What did you learn from the experience?

Chapter 39

- Why do you think Zero chooses this moment to confess about the stolen shoes?

Chapter 40

- Why is Stanley surprised to find the sack of jars and the shovel so far down the mountain?

Chapter 41

- Zero says, "If I had just kept those old smelly sneakers, then neither of us would be here right now." Do you think he's right? Is there anything positive about their situation?

Chapter 42

- Stanley believes it was his destiny to be hit by those falling shoes. What's the difference between coincidence and destiny? Do you believe in destiny?

Chapter 43

- When he hears Zero's stories, how does Stanley feel about his own family? How do these stories make you feel?

Chapter 44

- How do you think Stanley and Zero feel when the Warden confronts them?

Chapter 45

- What do you learn about the Warden in this chapter? How does it influence your feelings about her?

Chapter 46

- Why do you think Zero gives Stanley the thumbs-up sign?

Chapter 47

- The Warden's name is Walker; who else in the story has the same last name? Why might this be important?

Chapter 48

- Why won't Stanley leave without Hector?

Chapter 49

- The chapter ends with these words: "... and for the first time in over a hundred years, a drop of rain fell into the empty lake." Does this seem important to you? Why do you suppose the author chose to end Part II here?

Chapter 50

- How has Stanley changed in the course of the story? Do you think Stanley had a "hole" in his life before attending Camp Green Lake? Does he have one now?

"Stanley was not a bad kid. He was innocent of the crime for which he was convicted. He'd just been in the wrong place at the wrong time."

—Holes

When your name is Stanley Yelnats, bad luck just seems to run in the family. Stanley's great-grandfather, the first Stanley Yelnats, lost his fortune to an outlaw called Kissin' Kate Barlow. Stanley's father is a luckless inventor whose experiments keep failing. And now Stanley IV, our Stanley, has been wrongly convicted of a crime he didn't commit: stealing a pair of athletic shoes. So Stanley doesn't seem too surprised to find himself headed off to a detention camp for bad boys in the middle of the Texas desert.

Camp Green Lake takes its name from a lake that dried up more than a hundred years ago. The camp is run by a sinister person called the Warden. (Stanley is told, "There's only one rule at Camp Green Lake: Don't upset the Warden.") The Warden's second in command, Mr. Sir, introduces Stanley to life at the camp: "You are to dig one hole each day, including Saturdays and Sundays. Each hole must be five feet deep, and five feet across in every direction. Your shovel is your measuring stick. Breakfast is served at 4:30." This punishment supposedly builds character, but Stanley soon figures out the real reason for all the digging: The Warden is searching for something buried in the lakebed.

Stanley is assigned to Group D, run by a counselor named Mr. Pendanski, otherwise known as Mom. Nearly everyone at Camp Green Lake has a nickname, and Stanley soon becomes Caveman. At first Stanley seems to adjust well to camp life. The work is exhausting and the shoveling gives him terrible blisters, but he gradually grows stronger. "He figured that in a year and a half he'd be either in great physical condition, or else dead." As an accepted member of Group D, Stanley even begins to enjoy a sense of belonging he has never known before.

Then one day Stanley unearths something interesting: a small golden tube engraved with the initials KB. As promised, he turns the cylinder over to X-Ray, the group's leader; X-Ray pretends to find it in his own hole and hands it over to the Warden, hoping for a reward. It's clear that the tube is a clue to what lies buried at the bottom of Green Lake, but Stanley knows "whatever they were looking for, they were looking in the wrong place."

As it happens, the tube comes from a lipstick that belonged to Kissin' Kate Barlow, the outlaw who robbed Stanley's great-grandfather and left him stranded in the desert. This is just one of many coincidences that occur in *Holes*. (A coincidence is a chance happening or meeting.) Sachar braids his plot together from three different story lines, or narratives, two of which occur in the past. Part of the fun of reading this book is seeing how cleverly the author brings these different story lines together.

One of the stories from the past concerns Stanley's great-great-grandfather Elya. This narrative may remind you of a folktale, because it uses many of the elements of this kind of story. As a young man in Latvia, Elya made a promise to a woman named Madame Zeroni. In return for her help, Elya agreed to fulfill three tasks: He would carry Madame Zeroni up a mountain, help her drink from a magical stream, and sing her a special song. But Elya forgets to keep his promise when he sails off to America, and the Yelnats family is cursed for generations to come.

The second story tells how a beautiful and kindhearted schoolteacher becomes a notorious outlaw. Katherine Barlow was the teacher in the town of Green Lake, before the lake dried up. Katherine fell in love with Sam, the onion man. Because she was white and Sam was black, their love had tragic consequences. Charles Walker, a man who wanted Katherine Barlow for himself, shot Sam to death. "Three days after Sam's death, Miss Katherine shot the sheriff while he was sitting in his chair drinking a cup of coffee. . . . For the next twenty years Kissin' Kate Barlow was one of the most feared outlaws in all the West." We also learn that Kissin' Kate buried her loot somewhere in the lakebed. She died from a yellow-spotted lizard bite before she could tell anyone where she'd hidden it.

More than a century later, the Warden wants desperately to find Kate's buried treasure. Meanwhile, Stanley has made a deal with a camper named Hector Zeroni, or Zero. In exchange for reading lessons, Zero will help Stanley dig his hole each day. This arrangement stirs up resentment among the other boys, who bring it to the Warden's attention. The Warden and Mr. Pendanski confront Stanley and Zero, demanding that the lessons stop. "It causes him stress," said Mr. Pendanski. "I know you mean well, Stanley, but face it. Zero's too stupid to learn to read." These insults are the last straw for Zero. He smashes his counselor in the face with a shovel and runs off into the desert.

As the chances for Zero's survival dwindle in the days that follow, Stanley can't ignore the nagging of his conscience. "What worried him the most, however, wasn't that it was too late. What worried him the most . . . was the fear that it *wasn't* too late." Finally Stanley escapes into the desert to search for Zero and, miraculously, finds him alive. They set off together toward a rock formation sticking up in the distance like a giant thumb. Stanley recalls that after being robbed by Kate Barlow, his great-grandfather claimed he "found refuge on God's thumb," and he hopes that Big Thumb may offer salvation to him and Zero, too.

Zero is so sick that Stanley has to carry him up the mountain. At the top, they find water to drink and wild onions to eat. As Zero sleeps, Stanley sings him a lullaby that his father used to sing to him. Without realizing it, Stanley has succeeded in fulfilling the promise his great-great-grandfather Elya failed to keep.

In the shadow of Big Thumb, Stanley and Zero eat onions and regain their strength. They decide to sneak back to camp and find the treasure still believed to be buried there. Unfortunately, the Warden catches them in the act and demands that they hand over the metal suitcase they have unearthed. The hole where the suitcase was buried turns out to be a nest of deadly yellow-spotted lizards, which swarm all over Stanley and Zero. The boys don't move and the Warden and the counselors don't grab the loot for fear of being bitten. This standoff lasts until the law arrives. The Attorney General of Texas and a lawyer named Ms. Morengo, hired by Stanley's father, show up with the news that Stanley has been cleared and is free to go. The Warden claims the suitcase belongs to her, but Zero can read the letters on its side, which spell out STANLEY YELNATS.

However, Stanley won't leave Camp Green Lake without Zero. During their ordeal in the desert, the boys formed a real friendship. Since Mr. Pendanski has erased Zero's files from the computer system, Stanley knows his friend is in danger of being erased, too. The Attorney General can't even determine why Zero has been sent to the camp, so the two boys get to leave Camp Green Lake along with the metal suitcase.

Stanley and Zero inadvertently succeed in bringing the whole brutal system of the camp to an end. As they leave the camp, Ms. Morengo gives Stanley more good news: His father has invented a wonderful product that smells like peaches and eliminates foot odor. At the book's conclusion there is reason to hope that both Stanley's family and Zero will lead better lives, thanks in part to the contents of the suitcase.

Thinking about the plot

- What are the different stories told in *Holes*? How do these stories relate to one another?
- What is the relationship of the past to the present in this book?
- What types of holes exist in the story?

> "There is no lake at Camp Green Lake.
> There once was a very large lake
> here, the largest lake in Texas. That
> was over a hundred years ago. Now it
> is just a dry, flat wasteland.
>
> "There used to be a town of Green
> Lake as well. The town shriveled and
> dried up along with the lake, and the
> people who lived there."
>
> —*Holes*

You can tell that setting is important in *Holes* because that is where the author begins. At first glance, this setting seems like a realistic place: somewhere in the Texas desert, in the present time. However, the novel constantly reminds us that appearances can be deceiving. In the world of *Holes*, the reader soon discovers that the real and the imaginary coexist and sometimes even blur together.

Sachar locates Camp Green Lake in a dry lakebed in Texas, a place where no rain has fallen in more than a century. The punishing heat and uncomfortable conditions make this the perfect spot for a prison. No guard towers or fences are necessary because anyone attempting to run away would quickly die of thirst and end up as "buzzard food," as Mr. Sir puts it. The only animals that can survive here are dangerous desert creatures: scorpions, rattlesnakes, and the deadly yellow-spotted lizards that everyone fears.

However, Green Lake wasn't always dry, which is something else we learn in the revealing opening paragraph. The fossil fish that Stanley digs up serves as a reminder that this was once a beautiful lake, which "sparkled like a giant emerald in the sun." *Holes* contains three stories, all intersecting in one place. One of these stories tells how the lake, and the town named after it, became a wasteland.

Stanley's first impressions of Camp Green Lake sketch out a stark picture for the reader: "The land was barren and desolate. He could see a few rundown buildings and some tents. Farther away there was a cabin beneath two tall trees. Those two trees were the only plant life he could see. There weren't even weeds." Sachar, who lives in Austin, says that the blistering Texas summers gave him the first ideas for this book. On Stanley's second day at the camp, "The only thing that got him out of bed was knowing that every second he wasted meant he was one step closer to the rising of the sun. He hated the sun."

These descriptive details seem realistic enough, but there are also signs that Camp Green Lake is not an actual place. Pockmarked with holes, the dry lakebed reminds Stanley of the surface of the moon, an unearthly setting. The yellow-spotted lizards we hear about do not really exist but are inventions of the author. Big Thumb, the strange rock formation where Stanley's great-grandfather found refuge in the desert, marks a spot where water miraculously runs uphill. This magical spring irrigates a secret onion field, the source of a tonic that supposedly can cure illness and prolong life. According to Sam, the onion man, a steady diet of onions has helped his donkey, Mary Lou. She lived to be almost fifty, "extraordinarily old for a donkey."

The combination of realistic details and imaginary elements in the setting of this book may remind you of a fable or a folktale, demonstrating how Sachar borrows from these traditions in *Holes*. Folk narratives typically include both real and fanciful elements (think of the Paul Bunyan stories, for instance), and are part of the culture of the American West.

In the stories in *Holes* that take place in the past, things are not what they appear to be, either. The town of Green Lake seems too good to be true—and it is. The narrator first describes it as a "heaven on earth" where the sky is "painted pale blue and pink— the same color as the lake and the peach trees along its shore." Like the mirage that confuses Stanley in the desert, making him believe that he sees a pool of water as he searches for Zero, the placid little town of Green Lake is a beautiful vision that disappears when we look more closely. Before long, we witness the ugliness of racism and violence that lurks beneath the surface of the community.

Finally, in this book we must remember that what isn't there is as important as what is. A hole, after all, is a space where something is missing, and this is also true of Camp Green Lake. Read the first paragraphs of the book again and you'll hear more about what is missing from this setting than what is there. The absence of water influences much of what happens to Stanley at the camp. As Mr. Sir makes clear, the lack of water means that escape from Camp Green Lake is practically impossible: "Nobody runs away from here. We don't need a fence. Know why? Because we've got the only water for a hundred miles."

Thinking about the setting

- Where does *Holes* take place?
- Which parts of the setting seem realistic to you? Which ones do not?
- How does the setting influence what happens in the story?

"The reader might find it interesting that Stanley's father invented his cure for foot odor the day after the great-great-grandson of Elya Yelnats carried the great-great-great-grandson of Madame Zeroni up the mountain."

—*Holes*

"Whatever goes around, comes around"

This expression means that, over time, all human actions have appropriate consequences: Bad deeds are eventually punished, and good deeds ultimately rewarded. A more complicated version of this theme plays out repeatedly in the plot of *Holes*. The family curse of the Yelnatses, the fate of the town of Green Lake, and Stanley's willingness to risk his life for a friend, all show that in life, things come full circle. Throughout the story, objects from the past keep turning up. The fossil fish Stanley unearths, Sam's rowboat, Katherine's lipstick tube and spiced peaches, and Stanley's great-grandfather's fortune are all reminders that nothing stays buried forever, especially the truth.

After Elya Yelnats forgets his promise to Madame Zeroni and sets sail for America, he is plagued by misfortune. "Elya worked hard, but bad luck seemed to follow him everywhere. He always seemed to be in the wrong place at the wrong time." Back in Latvia, Madame Zeroni had warned Elya that if he failed to keep his promise to her, "he and his descendants would be doomed for all of eternity." Sachar leaves it to the reader to decide whether curses really have any power. But the facts are these: Trouble haunts the Yelnats family until Stanley manages to fulfill the terms of his great-great-grandfather's promise by carrying Hector Zeroni up the mountain.

Elya's failure to keep his promise results from his forgetfulness. Like his descendant Stanley, he is a good-hearted, well-meaning young man, and when he realizes his mistake, he feels genuinely sorry. "He wasn't afraid of the curse. He thought that was a lot of nonsense. He felt bad because he knew Madame Zeroni had wanted to drink from the stream before she died." In comparison, the lynching of Sam is a much more terrible offense. The citizens of the town of Green Lake condemn Katherine and Sam—a white woman and a black man—for daring to fall in love. After Sam's brutal murder, rain stops falling on Green Lake. When the lake that sustained the community eventually evaporates, so does the town. A century later, Trout Walker's descendant, the Warden, must still pay for her ancestor's crimes.

Good deeds create a kind of fallout, too. By agreeing to teach Zero to read, Stanley ensures they will both escape the Warden's clutches when Zero correctly identifies the name on the metal suitcase. When he commits himself to stealing the water truck and takes off in search of his friend, Stanley finally seizes control of his own destiny, assumes responsibility for another person, and sets in motion a series of events that results in the closing of the camp.

Inheritance

A related theme in *Holes* is inheritance, or what gets passed down from one generation to the next within a family. This may mean everything from money and property to physical characteristics like eye or hair color, or even things that aren't visible, such as responsibilities and character traits. You've probably noticed that many of the characters in *Holes* are related to one another. Characters in the stories that take place in the past turn out to be ancestors of characters in the present. This gives the reader a chance to see how the process of inheritance plays out over time.

The book's main character, Stanley Yelnats IV, has a name that has been passed down for generations within his family. In the Yelnats household, it's a family joke to blame anything bad that happens on "Stanley's no-good-dirty-rotten-pig-stealing-great-great-grandfather," the alleged source of the family curse. This curse is supposedly why Stanley's great-grandfather lost his fortune in the desert, Stanley's father perpetually fails as an inventor, and Stanley gets shipped off to detention camp.

While Stanley may believe his bad luck stems from being a Yelnats, his family also affords him certain advantages. One feature of the family legacy is a certain kind of optimism:

"Despite their awful luck, they always remained hopeful. As Stanley's father liked to say, 'I learn from failure.'" This hopefulness enables Stanley to persevere even when things look bleak.

While he has no friends at school, Stanley is rescued from real loneliness by the love of his parents. His mother's letter cheers him up at camp; he has happy recollections of his father singing him a lullaby that has been passed down in his family for generations. When Stanley finds himself in the lizards' nest and expects to die at any minute, he finds comfort in memories from his childhood.

Zero, on the other hand, is mostly alone in the world until the book's conclusion. He has inherited the penetrating eyes and piercing intelligence of his great-great-great-grandmother Madame Zeroni, along with a smile too big for his face. Before abandoning him in a park, his mother taught Zero how to provide for himself: "'We always took what we needed,' Zero said. 'When I was little, I didn't even know it was *stealing*. I don't remember when I found out.'"

In *Holes,* Zero, a homeless African-American kid with no family to care about what happens to him, can be erased without a trace, which is exactly what the Warden plans to do. Stanley may be poor but compared with Zero he has many advantages, starting with his skin color.

Another case of inheritance in the book concerns the Warden, Ms. Walker. She is related to Charles "Trout" Walker, the wealthy son of the family who owned land around Green Lake. The Warden has inherited the task of searching for Kate Barlow's buried loot: "When I was little I'd watch my parents dig holes, every weekend and holiday. When I got bigger, I had to dig, too. Even on Christmas." Finding this out may make you feel a little differently about this character. Ultimately Ms. Walker has to sell her family's land after the camp is closed down.

Bullying

Bullying is another important theme in *Holes*. A boy named Derrick Dunne bullies Stanley at the middle school they both attend. "The teachers never took Stanley's complaints seriously, because Derrick was so much smaller than Stanley." However, bullies are not necessarily larger than their victims; a bully can be anyone who tries to frighten, intimidate, or torment another person by using physical threats, teasing, or other forms of verbal abuse.

This book also shows that bullying doesn't just happen between kids, but can occur between adults as well. Stanley witnesses the Warden bullying both Mr. Pendanski and Mr. Sir. An adult may also bully a child, as Mr. Pendanski does with Zero, constantly picking on him and insulting him. Mr. Pendanski never misses a chance to tell Zero how stupid and worthless he is. When the counselor finds out that Stanley has been giving Zero reading lessons, he says scornfully, "You might as well try to teach this shovel to read! It's got more brains than Zero." Stanley is also bullied at camp, especially by Mr. Sir and by a boy named Zigzag.

As Stanley begins to feel accepted by the other campers in his group, he has revenge fantasies. "Stanley played the scene over and over again in his mind, each time watching another boy from Group D beat up Derrick Dunne." If you have ever been bullied at school or in your neighborhood, you can probably identify with Stanley and his daydreams.

Being bullied can be a terrible experience, and the sense of powerlessness and humiliation it causes may be hard to forget. Ironically, Derrick Dunne is ultimately responsible for clearing Stanley, by giving him an alibi. Dunne tells Ms. Morengo, the attorney, that Stanley was in the boys' bathroom at the time of the crime, trying to retrieve his notebook from the toilet: "Stanley felt his ears redden. Even after everything he'd been through, the memory still caused him to feel shame."

Thinking about the themes

- What do you think is the main theme of *Holes*? What are some other themes in the book?
- What are some of the things—either positive or negative—that have been passed down in your family?
- Have you ever bullied anyone, or been the victim of a bully?

Characters: Who Are These People, Anyway?

Since there are a few different story lines in this book, there are a lot of different characters, many of whom are related to one another or whose lives somehow cross. The main characters are Stanley Yelnats and Hector Zeroni ("Zero").

Here is a list of characters, divided into those in the present and those in the past. Following that is a brief description of each of the two main characters.

Characters in the present

Stanley Yelnats IV	tall, heavy, camper in Group D, main character
Hector Zeroni ("Zero")	small camper in Group D
X-Ray	leader of the Group D campers, wears thick glasses
Armpit	tall camper in Group D
Magnet	camper in Group D
Zigzag	Group D camper with frizzy blond hair
Squid	camper in Group D
Twitch	fidgety camper in Group D
Mr. Pendanski	counselor for Group D

The Warden, Ms. Walker	woman who runs Camp Green Lake
Mr. Sir	camp director
Stanley's father	inventor
Stanley's mother	homemaker
Derrick Dunne	middle-school bully
Clyde "Sweet Feet" Livingston	famous baseball player
Ms. Morengo	patent attorney
Attorney General	head lawyer for the state of Texas

Characters in the past

In Latvia

Elya Yelnats	Stanley's great-great-grandfather
Myra Menke	beautiful but empty-headed girl
Madame Zeroni	Zero's great-great-great-grandmother
Myra's father	decides who Myra will marry

In America

Sarah Miller	Stanley IV's great-great-grandmother
Katherine Barlow	a.k.a. Kissin' Kate, schoolteacher turned outlaw
Sam	"Onion Sam," an onion seller
Mary Lou	Sam's donkey
Charles "Trout" Walker	rich man
Linda Walker	Trout's wife

Stanley Yelnats: The protagonist, or main character, of *Holes*, Stanley, is a quiet, friendless boy who has grown up in a poor family with loving parents. You may have noticed that many of the characters in the book have a "signature"—a habit, gesture, or phrase they repeat throughout the story, which tells you something important about them. (For example, how many times does Mr. Sir say, "This isn't a Girl Scout camp"?) Stanley's signature is his shrug. When you read the book again, pay attention to how often the author mentions that "Stanley raised and lowered one shoulder." A shrug lets Stanley respond without really committing himself. Stanley often uses this gesture as a way to deal with other people. After the Warden scratches Mr. Sir with her poisonous fingernails, Stanley keeps quiet about what he witnessed in the cabin: "Out on the lake, the other boys asked Stanley what he knew about Mr. Sir's face, but he just shrugged and dug his hole. If he didn't talk about it, maybe it would go away."

At the middle school he attends, Stanley gets teased for being overweight. He has no friends and although he is big, Stanley is frequently bullied by smaller kids. Even his teachers treat him unkindly. Stanley can't seem to stick up for himself, which is one reason he winds up at Camp Green Lake.

Stanley comes from a poor family. Unsuccessful inventors like Stanley's father don't earn much money, and Stanley and his parents are "crammed in a tiny apartment" because they cannot afford a bigger home. As a child, Stanley had fantasized about going to summer camp, a luxury beyond his family's means. When Stanley is sent to Camp Green Lake, he and his parents "tried to pretend that he was just going away to camp for a while, just like rich kids do."

It's clear that Stanley has been raised in a loving environment, and he is a loving and dutiful son. He promises his mother that he will write home once a week, and he keeps that promise. *"Today was my first day at camp, and I've already made some friends. We've been out on the lake all day, so I'm pretty tired. . . ."* The little lies that Stanley tells in his letters from camp seem to be as much for his mother's benefit as for his own: He doesn't want her to worry about him. When Stanley thinks he may die at Camp Green Lake, his main concern is how this will affect his folks: "For him, at least, it would be over. For his parents, the pain would never end."

In the Yelnats family, bad luck is an inherited trait, but so is the ability to remain hopeful. His hope that Zero may still be alive prompts Stanley to set out after him: "*It's too late*, he told himself. Zero couldn't have survived. *But what if it wasn't too late?*" Hope keeps Stanley heading toward Big Thumb, even when all logic says there can be no water there.

Stanley's decision to go after Zero is a critical moment in the evolution of his character. His willingness to commit himself to Zero, the first real friend he has ever had, shows us that Stanley is finally capable of taking control of his own destiny.

Hector Zeroni ("Zero"): Like Stanley, Zero is sent to Camp Green Lake for stealing a pair of shoes. (As it turns out, he actually stole the shoes Stanley is accused of stealing.) A homeless African-American boy abandoned by his mother in a city park, Zero is a thief by necessity rather than by choice. While at first Zero might seem like a minor character, he becomes important in the second half of the book when a friendship develops between Stanley and him.

If Stanley's signature is a shrug, Zero's signature is his silence. When you reread *Holes*, notice how often the narrator tells you "Zero said nothing." By repeatedly calling attention to Zero's silence, Sachar makes the reader very aware of it.

Zero is the smallest of the campers in Group D. His size and his silence make him easy to overlook. Everyone at Camp Green Lake underestimates Zero, especially Mr. Pendanski. While the counselor appears friendly enough at first, his true nature emerges in response to Zero. "You know why his name's Zero?" asks Mr. Pendanski. "Because there's nothing inside his head." Even Stanley dismisses Zero at first: "He didn't care what Zero thought. Zero was nobody."

Zero turns out to be extremely smart, however. Although he cannot read, he has a natural talent for mathematics that quickly impresses Stanley. One early clue to Zero's intelligence is his eyes, which seem to look right into people's souls. In fact, Zero has the same dark and penetrating eyes as his great-great-great-grandmother, Madame Zeroni. "When she looked at you, her eyes seemed to expand, and you felt like she was looking right through you." Zero can see right through Mr. Pendanski's act and recognize him for the heartless person he really is. "If anybody had X-Ray vision, it was Zero."

When Stanley finally agrees to give him reading lessons, Zero makes rapid progress. By the end of the book Zero can read well enough to know that the letters on the suitcase spell out Stanley's name.

As the relationship between the two boys develops, Zero proves he can be a loyal, brave, and generous friend. He defends Stanley from Zigzag's attack even though he is much smaller than Zigzag. Later, when Stanley finds him under the overturned rowboat, Zero gives Stanley half of his last jar of sploosh. When they climb out of the lakebed, Zero helps hoist Stanley out with his shovel, even though it means injuring his own hands.

Zero's memories of his childhood make up some of the saddest passages in *Holes*. Up on the mountain Zero tells Stanley about the day his mother disappeared.

> "And then one day she didn't come back," Zero said. His voice sounded suddenly hollow. "I waited for her at Laney Park."
>
> "Laney Park," said Stanley. "I've been there."
>
> "You know the playscape?" asked Zero.
>
> "Yeah. I've played on it."
>
> "I waited there for more than a month," said Zero. "You know that tunnel that you crawl through, between the slide and the swinging bridge? That's where I slept."

Yet despite these hardships, Zero shows that he, like Stanley, can still be hopeful, even under the worst circumstances. "When you spend your whole life living in a hole," he said, "the only way you can go is up."

Thinking about the characters

- Why is Stanley nicknamed "Caveman"? How does his character change over the course of the book?
- How does Zero's character change?
- What are the "signatures" of the other characters? What do they tell you about them?
- Do the characters in the past seem as real or complex to you as those in the present? Why or why not?

Everybody digs this book!

Holes is the winner of the 1999 Newbery Medal. Of all the
children's books published each year in the United States, only
one book earns this prize. The Newbery Medal honors the finest
contributions to American literature for children, and the
children's librarians of the American Library Association choose
each year's winner. A Newbery book displays a bronze medal on
its cover, a visible symbol of its literary excellence that has a
huge impact on book sales. Newbery authors are flooded with
invitations to read and sign their books. After winning the award,
Louis Sachar found himself very much in demand. The Newbery
Medal is just one of a dozen honors that *Holes* has earned. Look
inside the front cover of your book for a list of all the awards.

During the spring of 2002, all the kids in Seattle, Washington,
had their noses buried in *Holes,* the first book chosen for a new
citywide reading program called "What If All Kids Read the Same
Book?" This program is a version of the nationally known adult
reading program that encourages everyone in one city to read
and discuss the same book. Sachar's novel was translated into
Hebrew and Chinese and converted into Braille, a system of
reading for the blind, for the program. The judges who selected
Holes decided that the book, which was already popular with

children and adults, would appeal to a whole range of readers and encourage a lot of worthwhile discussion.

Stanley Yelnats, folk hero?

Boston Globe–Horn Book Award judge Maria B. Salvadore, one of the judges who selected *Holes* as a winner from thousands of submissions, has called Stanley Yelnats an "unlikely but likable folk hero." A folk hero is usually an ordinary person who accomplishes something extraordinary to help or inspire other people. Some real-life American folk heroes you may have heard of include Johnny Appleseed, Sojourner Truth, and Woody Guthrie. Paul Bunyan and Pecos Bill are some fictional folk heroes you may be familiar with.

Putting the pieces together

In the *New York Times Book Review*, Betsy Hearne called *Holes* "a smart jigsaw puzzle of a novel," and praised the book's intricate plot in which different truths are revealed to the reader and to Stanley, but not always at the same time. As Hearne pointed out, "Every revelation of the past ups the ante of the present."

Bringing *Holes* to the stage and screen

Spotlight on Stanley! *Holes* is a story in which nothing is quite what it seems, so what better place to explore the deceptive nature of appearances than in a theater? The Seattle Children's Theatre staged the book as a play, based on a script written by Louis Sachar, which opened in April 2002 to favorable reviews.

Much-loved books are often adapted for the screen, and *Holes* is no exception. A movie version of the novel came out in April 2003 starring Shia LaBeouf as Stanley, Khleo Thomas as Zero, Sigourney Weaver as the Warden, and Patricia Arquette as Kissin' Kate Barlow. Louis Sachar wrote the screenplay for the film.

Survivor: The Texas desert

When the film version of *Holes* came out, Sachar's publisher issued a companion book: *Stanley Yelnats's Survival Guide to Camp Green Lake.* Be sure to read it before you plan a camping trip in the Texas desert.

Thinking about what others think about *Holes*

- Do you think *Holes* deserved to win the Newbery Medal? Have you read other Newbery Medal–winning books? How do they compare?
- Do you think *Holes* was a good choice for a citywide reading program? What other books that you've read might make good candidates for this program?
- Would you agree that Stanley qualifies as a folk hero? What might make him an "unlikely" hero?
- Can you identify specific moments in the plot of *Holes* in which something we learn about the past changes the meaning of what is happening in the present?

Glossary

Here are some words used in *Holes*. Some may be new to you or used in new ways.

authenticated proved that something is real and genuine

custody control exercised by a person or an authority; the legal right to look after a child

defective imperfect or flawed

delirious confused and babbling

delirium a kind of mental disturbance, often accompanied by hallucinations

despicable deserving to be disliked

grotesque very strange or ugly

hallucinations imagined things that aren't really there; delusions

incarcerated imprisoned; locked up

initiate to introduce or start something new

jurisdiction authority or control

legitimate lawful

mirage an optical effect that makes you think you see something in the distance, like water, that is not really there

paranoid irrationally suspicious and distrustful of others

patent attorney a lawyer specializing in the rights to inventions

perseverance not giving up, even when faced with obstacles and difficulties

precarious dangerously unstable

promissory note a written promise to pay someone a certain amount of money, like an IOU

pursuant to legal phrase meaning "according to"

refuge a place providing protection or shelter

stifling cutting off circulation or smothering

strenuous vigorously active

sundial a device for determining the time of day using sunlight. A pointer casts a shadow that moves slowly around a flat, marked dial.

tedious tiring and boring

ward a young person under the protection of the court

warden an official in charge of the operation of a prison

Louis Sachar on Writing

"Every time you write you learn from your writing."

—Louis Sachar

Stanley Yelnats, the quiet hero of *Holes*, has learned to keep his mouth shut, since he believes that unpleasant things have a way of becoming more real when you talk about them. Stanley's creator, Louis Sachar, also uses silence as a strategy. "I never talk about a book until I'm finished writing it," Sachar says. "I think that is helpful for writing, as well as for anything else that takes a lot of self-motivation. The more you talk about something, the less you tend to do it."

Each morning, Sachar holes up in his study to write. His dogs, Tippy and Lucky, stand guard, ready to growl at anyone who tries to disturb Sachar while he's working. "Writing is a kind of self-hypnosis," he says. "Interruptions break the spell, and it's sometimes hard to get it back."

Sachar writes for about two hours before he "runs out of steam." It's amazing what he manages to accomplish in that relatively short amount of time. So far he has written twenty-one books this way!

A book may begin with just a little idea, sometimes just a character trait. Sachar says that most of his ideas come from what he remembers "doing and feeling and thinking as a child." He doesn't plan or outline his stories in advance, so he doesn't know what will happen next. Each story goes through a series of rewrites before Sachar feels satisfied with it.

"I write five or six drafts of each of my books. With each draft, the story changes and the ideas are transformed. What amazes me is that most days feel useless. I don't seem to accomplish anything—just a few pages, most of which don't seem very good. Yet, when I put all those wasted days together, I somehow end up with a book of which I'm very proud."

Until now, all of Sachar's books have been written for children. But *Holes* appeals to both kids and grown-ups. Now Sachar wonders whether he should try his hand at writing something intended for adults. That's one way to make sure that your audience never outgrows your books!

- **Your writing process:** Every writer has a *process:* a way of working that is most productive for that individual. Some people write best at night; others feel more creative in the afternoon. One writer needs absolute quiet; another likes a little background music. Louis Sachar is a morning writer, and at the start of each day he spends two uninterrupted hours working on his latest project. That may not seem like much to you—after all, the average adult workday is eight hours or more—but so far Sachar has managed to finish a shelf full of books this way!

What is your writing process? You probably already have a sense of when and where you work best. Write a paragraph or two describing your writing process in as much detail as possible. At what time of day are you most productive? Do you write on the computer or in longhand with a pen and paper? Do you like to be near a window, or maybe even outdoors? Do you need a beverage at your elbow to sip while you're writing? Do you write multiple drafts? Next time you have a writing assignment for school, be aware of your own writing process and try to create the right environment for your best work.

- **Creating a guidebook:** In Chapter 5 of *Holes* we learn, "There's really only one rule at Camp Green Lake: Don't upset the Warden." But there are other rules for surviving in this harsh environment, such as if you don't bother rattlesnakes and scorpions, they won't bother you—usually, that is. Write a guide for an unlucky camper headed for Camp Green Lake. What does that person need to know in order to survive there?

• **The Zeroni family reunion:** At the end of *Holes*, Zero (Hector) is accompanied by a woman we can assume to be his mother. "A woman sitting in the chair behind Hector was absentmindedly fluffing his hair with her fingers. She wasn't very old, but her skin had a weathered look to it, almost like leather. Her eyes seemed weary, as if she'd seen too many things in her life that she didn't want to see. And when she smiled, her mouth seemed too big for her face." Imagine what the reunion between these two characters might have been like, how and where and when it took place, and what each person said and did. You might want to write it in prose, as a continuation of the book, or imagine it in a different form: a scene from a play or movie, a poem, or the lyrics to a song.

• **What's your signature?:** Many of the characters in *Holes* have a *signature:* an identifying trait or mannerism that tells you something important about them, such as X-Ray's filthy glasses or Onion Sam's phrase "I can fix that." The people you know probably have signatures, too (your uncle Ed's Yosemite Sam mud flaps may speak volumes about him!). If you were a character in a book, what do you think *your* signature might be? Would it be a gesture, a phrase, an object, an article of clothing, or something else? Write a page or two describing yourself as if you were a character in a book and incorporate your signature into that description.

- **Tell a tall tale:** Part of what makes *Holes* such a good read is the way Sachar weaves together realism and fantasy, by including elements from fables and folktales in his story. Tall tales are a popular form of folktale in the United States. Find out about the characteristics of this kind of narrative by reading some tall tales. Good collections include *Tall Tale America: A Legendary History of Our Humorous Heroes* by Walter Blair and *American Tall Tales* by Mary Pope Osborne. Pay attention to how the writers of these tales use exaggeration to create humor. Watch for repetition of phrases and themes, and notice how animals often function as helpers. Then, try writing a tall tale of your own.

- **Wordplay:** "Stanley Yelnats" is a palindrome, spelled the same both forward and backward. Other palindromes include the words *mom, radar,* and *racecar,* and the names *Elle, Anna,* and *Otto.* Whole phrases can be palindromes, too, such as "A daffodil slid off Ada" and "Rats live on no evil star." You can find more palindromes in Jon Agee's book *Go Hang a Salami! I'm a Lasagna Hog!: and Other Palindromes.* Come up with some palindromes of your own, or make your name into a palindrome. You might also want to check out some of the Web sites devoted to palindromes like www.palindromes.com, www.fun-with-words.com, or www.mockok.com, to see how inventive people can get with this kind of wordplay.

- **What's in a name?:** "There is no lake at Camp Green Lake." Places are often named for things that no longer exist: Go down to Canal Street in New York City and you won't find anything that looks even remotely like a canal! Make a list of some places in your town or city named for features of the landscape that are no longer there.

- **Be a tutor:** When Stanley agrees to teach Zero to read, he learns even more in return and he makes a friend, too. Consider volunteering to tutor a fellow student in a subject you especially enjoy. You can offer to work after school with someone who might benefit from extra homework help. Besides, teaching somebody else is a great way to improve your own skills or knowledge.

• **Be inventive:** Stanley's father is an inventor who wants to find a way to recycle old sneakers. Eventually he stumbles on the solution to another problem: how to get rid of foot odor! Brainstorm a list of inventions you think would improve the world. If you come up with any really fantastic ideas, you might want to find out about the patenting process. The United States Patent and Trademark Office has a Web site for kids (www.uspto.gov/go/kids). Another good site for young inventors is www.kids.patentcafe.com.

• **Mock trial:** Put the Warden on trial! Enlist friends or family members who have read *Holes* to act as attorneys for the defense and the prosecution. Assemble evidence, call witnesses, argue each side of the case—you've probably seen enough TV shows that take place in courtrooms (*Court TV*, *Judging Amy*, *Law and Order*, *The Practice*, to name just a few) to have a basic idea of how the legal process works. Should you let the Warden testify on her own behalf? Find a friend who hasn't read *Holes* to act as an impartial judge, and let her or him reach a verdict based on the strength of the case each side presents.

• **Make your own sploosh!:** "Every summer Miss Katherine would pick bushels of peaches and preserve them in jars with cinnamon, cloves, nutmeg, and other spices...." Zero calls the sweet, muddy liquid he finds in jars under the rowboat "sploosh," and it helps keep him alive in the desert after he runs away from camp. Here's a recipe to help you and an adult re-create Kate Barlow's prize-winning spiced peaches.

Kissin' Kate Barlow's Spiced Peaches

Ingredients

1 can (29 ounces) peach halves, drained (save the syrup in
   a separate bowl)

2/3 cup apple cider vinegar

1 cup light brown sugar, packed

1/4 teaspoon salt

8 whole cloves

1 cinnamon stick

1/4 teaspoon ground nutmeg

Directions

In a saucepan, combine 2/3 cup of the peach syrup with all the other ingredients except the peaches. Simmer uncovered for 10 minutes.

Pour over peaches. Cool, then cover and chill for at least 24 hours (or 110 years!).

Bring to room temperature and eat. Any leftover peaches will keep in the refrigerator for a week.

Serves 6.

- **Buried treasure:** You can bury something fun or interesting for someone in the future to discover, such as an old toy, an earring, a plastic bag full of pennies, or anything else you think might be fun for some future archaeologist to dig up. If you decide to bury an object that will decay, be sure to seal it in a watertight can or glass jar. You could also make a time capsule: Pack an empty coffee can or a pickle jar with some photographs, a newspaper, a tape or CD, a page from your journal, or anything else that helps capture the feeling of a particular point in history. Then, seal up your time capsule and bury it in the backyard, or just put it way back in a closet and promise yourself you won't open it for at least five years.

• **Wild women of the Wild West:** Kissin' Kate Barlow is a fictional character, but real female outlaws helped make the Old West an even wilder place. Visit your local library or go online to learn about the notorious Belle Starr, known as "the Bandit Queen"; Cattle Kate; the beautiful Etta Place, who teamed up with Butch Cassidy and the Sundance Kid; and other famous women outlaws.

• **Unearth your own family history:** Do you know where your great-grandparents were born, what kind of work they did, or how they died? Go through old photo albums and scrapbooks, read old letters and journals, interview the oldest people in your family, and find out as much as you can about your own roots. Write down any family stories, songs, or traditions you learn about in a special notebook, and create a record of your family's history to pass down to your descendants.

Other books by Louis Sachar

The Boy Who Lost His Face (1989)

Dogs Don't Tell Jokes (1991)

Johnny's in the Basement (1981)

Sixth Grade Secrets (1987)

Someday, Angeline (1983)

Stanley Yelnats's Survival Guide to Camp Green Lake (2003)

There's a Boy in the Girls' Bathroom (1987)

Series by Louis Sachar

The Marvin Redpost series (includes *Marvin Redpost: Kidnapped at Birth?*, *Marvin Redpost: Is He a Girl?*, and other titles)

The Wayside School series (*Sideways Stories from Wayside School*, *Wayside School Is Falling Down*, and other titles)

Books about friendship under difficult circumstances

Belle Prater's Boy by Ruth White

The Pinballs by Betsy Byars

Books about homeless and/or abandoned children

Heaven Eyes by David Almond

Jip: His Story by Katherine Paterson

Maniac Magee by Jerry Spinelli

Monkey Island by Paula Fox

Books about survival

Among the Hidden by Margaret Peterson Haddix

The Goats by Brock Cole

Hatchet by Gary Paulsen

My Side of the Mountain by Jean Craighead George

The Sign of the Beaver by Elizabeth George Speare

The True Confessions of Charlotte Doyle by Avi

What Jamie Saw by Carolyn Coman

Books that mix magic and realism

Skellig by David Almond

Tuck Everlasting by Natalie Babbitt

Folktales and tall tales

American Tall Tales by Mary Pope Osborne

Cut from the Same Cloth: American Women of Myth, Legend and Tall Tale by Robert D. San Souci

John Henry by Julius Lester

The People Could Fly: American Black Folktales by Virginia Hamilton

Other books set in Texas

Dancing in Cadillac Light by Kimberly Willis Holt

When Zachary Beaver Came to Town by Kimberly Willis Holt

Bibliography

Books

Sachar, Louis. *Holes*. New York: Farrar, Straus, and Giroux, 1998.

Interviews

Phone interview with Louis Sachar, September 9, 2002.

Newspapers and magazines

Austin Chronicle, "Louis Sachar: Top of His Class," by Barbara Strickland, February 26, 1999, pp. 34–36.

New York Times Book Review, "He Didn't Do It," by Betsy Hearne, November 15, 1998, p. 52.

Seattle Post-Intelligencer, "*Holes* Has Seattle Middle-Schoolers All on the Same Page," by Rebekah Denn, March 7, 2002, pp. D1, D3.

Web sites

Alexlibris: alexlibris.com/rev_holes.asp

Austin Chronicle: austinchronicle.com

The Book Report Network:
www.kidsreads.com/authors/au-sachar-louis.asp

Children's Book Council:
www.cbcbooks.org/html/louissachar.html

Educational Paperback Association:
www.edupaperback.org/authorbios/Sachar_Louis.html

Public Broadcasting System: www.pbs.org/newshour

Reading Matters: readingmatters.co.uk/books/holes.html